BORN BEAUTIFUL BIRACIAL

A Compilation of Children's Essays

by Tanya Hutchins

For Jenny,
Live your life to the
fullest!
Tanya Hutchins

Published by TP Rewards, LLC
8647 Richmond Highway #659
Alexandria, VA 22309
www.tp-rewards.com

Book design by TP Rewards, LLC.
Cover photo by Tanya Hutchins.
Uncredited photos are courtesy of the families of the
children

International Standard Book Number: 978-0-9860659-5-8
Library of Congress Control Number: 2014914470

Published in the United States of America

THIS BOOK IS DEDICATED TO MY GRANDFATHER, MILFORD
TUCKER, THE SON OF A HALF GERMAN, HALF NATIVE
AMERICAN MOTHER AND A BLACK FATHER;
AND TO MY COUSIN EVANDREA PARKER,
WHO IS INCLUDED IN THIS BOOK.

CONTENTS

INTRODUCTION

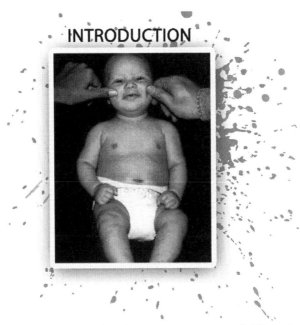

When I was young, my friends and I called people of different races "mixed." Now, they're called biracial. Whatever the label, these children, products of interracial marriages and unions, often grow up confused, not because of themselves necessarily, but because of society's perception and reaction to them.

There's a saying, "God doesn't make junk." All children are beautiful in God's eyes.

I offer this book as an inspiration to bi-racial, tri-racial, and multi-racial children everywhere. Please take the advice to heart and know that you are Born Beautiful Biracial!

My parents always told me that I had been adopted at age two. They also told me when I was younger what my racial background was. My mother was European- American and my father was European and African-American.

It was interesting growing up. There were six adopted kids in the family that I lived in. We had a family of eight kids (two of them were my mom's original kids). The rest of the kids in the family were mixed racially: I had two Korean sisters, a Native American sister, a brother who was Hispanic and another sister who was biracial like myself.

For many years, because I didn't know any better, I just I figured I was mulatto... I saw (the term) on TV, but back then "biracial" and "mixed race" weren't terms you heard very often. It raises a question in myself, "What are you?" and I always said that I was just mixed... black and white. But I'm really not just black and white... from the background that I understand I'm mostly white and kind of black.

I had an interesting experience one time. I was at a Nike play day in Chicago. I was meeting kids and signing autographs and this guy brought this little girl over who was about five years old. And he was so excited for her to meet me. When he introduced me he said, "This is Dan O'Brien. He won a gold medal. His mom was white and his dad was black."

FOREWORD
BY DAN O'BRIEN

He introduced me in a fashion that it's okay if you're mom and dad aren't the same color. It's okay; you can still turn out well. And I guess this child had a lot of trouble. She was from an all-black neighborhood and she was having a lot of difficulty.

And growing up, for me, it was always the opposite: I was always the darkest one in the crowd. So coming from the other perspective, I didn't really know that other side really existed: that black people didn't always accept mixed race people. All I knew was the life of a so-called black kid trying to fit into a white world.

You shouldn't have to choose. Be proud of who you are inside. I was really always looking for groups to fit into, and never really thought I found it until I became really secure with myself and said I'm an O'Brien. These are my parents, they raised me, they're white, regardless of what color I am and what color they are: this is who I am.

I think Born Beautiful Biracial is fantastic, because in this book somewhere, you're going to find someone you can associate with, relate to, and understand that maybe this person is experiencing the same thing you are.

Dan O'Brien
Olympic Gold Medalist

FOREWORD
BY DAN O'BRIEN

It's fun playing and finding other kids the same color & different colors as me.

I am half black and half white.

My dad is black and my mom is white.

I love both of (their) different colors but (they) like each other still.

All families are different.

We all love each other even though we are different and not the same color.

My brother Zac is white, my sister TiTi is kinda like me and my sister Ruthie is a little like me. I'm happy they are my family.

QUEEN AFRADESHIA JACOBS/ETZIONI
PHOENIX, ARIZONA
AGE 6

People should not make fun of my parents.

It doesn't matter that one is black and one is white.

People should be able to get married and to love each other.

There should not have been fighting in the "old" days about color.

The only advice that I have is to love your parents, they made you, and to love others.

It doesn't matter what you look like.

ASHLEY A. PORTER
ROUND ROCK, TEXAS
AGE 7

Being biracial is nothing to be ashamed of.

In fact, it is something to be proud of.

You were born with it, so be proud of it.

I think being biracial is fun because it makes me special.

Some people make fun of me. Sometimes I get mad, but I just say "I am proud of who I am" and just walk away or go on with what you were doing. Sometimes I could ignore them too.

Love,

BRANDON JETER
COLUMBUS, OHIO
AGE 8

TANYA HUTCHINS

TANYA HUTCHINS

HOW I FEEL WHEN PEOPLE ASK, "WHAT ARE YOU?"

People at first didn't ask me. So when I was in 2nd grade and kids started to ask, "What are you?" I was surprised. I told them I was multi-cultural... which meant my family had come from different cultures and different parts of the world to America.

I remember in Art class I had a tan crayon and we were doing self portraits when a boy sitting at my table said you have to use a black crayon. I went to the Teacher and said my skin isn't the color of this black crayon. She told me I should blend the tan and black together. I cried. My family told me I was beautiful and even went to talk with the teacher. She told me she was sorry but I still felt weird and hurt.

People don't ask much anymore. I am me: happy, smart, a good friend, caring and most of all I would like the world to think of biracial people and other races as just another wonderful person and not set people apart from other people. But, the point is I like myself. I like being Born Beautiful Biracial.

CHANDEL CHARLES
POWELL, OHIO
AGE 9

16

TANYA HUTCHINS

TANYA HUTCHINS

I am biracial because my mom is white and my dad is black. Being biracial is a good thing in our family because they all love us.

Sometimes being biracial can be different things to different people. For my brother and me it means different hair. I have curly hair. He has straight hair.

When my friends ask is that my dad, I just say yes. But most of them already know that he is my dad. I like it when people ask me that because I know that they think he is cool. Kids that are biracial are cool and if anyone teases you, it is because they do not have love in their heart.

TERIK MINOR
ANNAPOLIS, MD
AGE 9

18

TANYA HUTCHINS

19

I like being half Korean because it feels special because not a lot of people in America are half Korean. No one in my school that I know of is half Korean. A lot of people think I am Chinese. It makes me feel weird because I know I'm half Korean. I tell them that I am half Korean. Sometimes they are embarrassed because they didn't know.

I feel left out a little because I look different, but I know on the inside I am still the same as everyone else.

The bad thing about being half Korean is that I don't know any Korean words.

The good thing about being half Korean is that the food is good. I like being a little different than everyone else, it makes me feel special.

If I could give advice to someone who is half Korean, I would tell them that they may look different but they are still the same.

MADISON MOON
NEW ALBANY, OHIO
AGE 9

TANYA HUTCHINS

Being biracial is a gift. Being a different color is fun. What being biracial means to me, is like if my life was segregated I would be able to play with both because I am both; my dad is black, my mom is white and I came out just right.

If anyone asked me about my parents I would tell them that my Dad loved my Mom and so if you love someone that much you would marry them even if they are another color.

Being a different color makes me feel special. I am not too white and I am not too black and that makes me different. When I see (Irish Singer) Samantha Mumba, I feel lucky, as she is the same racial mix as me, and I look like her. It's nice to see other people that look like me, as I don't see too many.

If someone was having a hard time I would tell them that "you are special, beautiful and biracial. Not many people are biracial, that you have a gift, and not too many people have that gift."

AILISH ELZY
OAKLAND, CALIFORNIA
AGE 9

DENNIS GEANY

My mom is white and my dad is black.

I haven't seen him since I was born.

My mom got married when I was 8; he is a white man and he adopted me and now I have a half sister and brother.

I'm happy but a lot of times I feel different because they all have blond hair and blue eyes.

DANIELLE DERR
DRESHER, PENNSYLVANIA
AGE 10

My mom is Filipino and my Dad is German-Irish. I feel fortunate that God made me different because being the same isn't always a good thing. I am glad that I am different because I have a very unique skin color and I eat different foods. My favorite food from the Philippines is Chicken Adobo. I am also able to make new friends that are biracial at Filipino-American parties.

My advice to other biracial children is to remember that God made you in a very special way and you should be proud. Believe in yourself. God will always take care of you and give you the strength to stand tall. Make the best of being unique.

CAMILLE FROMMEYER
DUBLIN, OHIO
AGE 10

TANYA HUTCHINS

27

I am proud of all of my heritage. Even though I live in a mostly white community, I am still comfortable there. I also spend a lot of time with the black side of my family, and I am comfortable with them, too.

Once, though, one of my friends told me that in the Civil War, or segregation, that I would be considered black. I'm not sure about this.

EVY PARKER
CROTON, NEW YORK
AGE 10

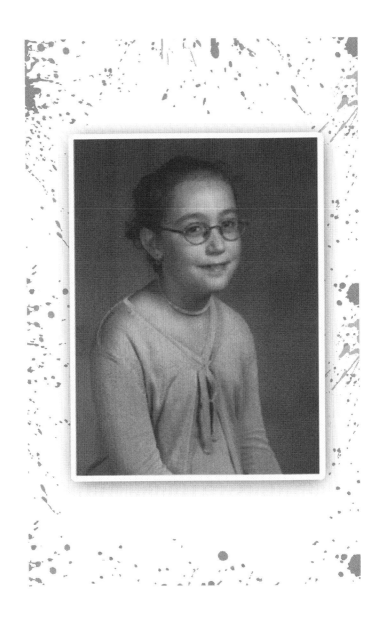

My mother is half-Japanese and half-White. My father is adopted and we don't really know what he is ethnically. So that makes me Japanese/White?

People don't think I look Japanese and it gets really annoying. But, I mean, I am Japanese and this is how I look - so this is what some Japanese people look like!

Some kids in my class say rude things to me about Japanese things such as culture and food, and I tell my mom. But, they don't think it up. It's on almost every TV show, even my favorite shows. Very few TV shows don't have one or two rude comments about Japanese things, like sushi.

My advice to other kids who are mixed is to tell people when they're wrong, and to talk about it with your parents.

MADELINE NAKASHIMA-CONWAY
OAKLAND, CALIFORNIA
AGE 10

I don't know why some people think that kids that are biracial are weird. All I know is that I'm happy because I have the best of both sides. But, as a kid, the one thing I want to do is have fun... not be treated like an alien. Maybe, by the time I grow up, the stupidity of thinking that because someone is different, you have the right to walk all over them (will be gone). Just try to be human first, then everything else.

ELI JOHNSON
COLUMBUS, OHIO
AGE 11

TANYA HUTCHINS

33

I go to a public middle school in the suburbs of New York City. I am multiracial, and very proud of it. Everyone is special, but being biracial is what makes me special.

I read a book on multiracial kids a couple of years ago. I liked it a lot because I learned about different people and how they dealt with bullying at their schools. I also liked that book because it talked about the word multiracial. So now, I can tell the difference between being multiracial and biracial.

My family is the best, and only, family I've ever had. Having a caring mom, who is Japanese- American, and a caring father who is African- American. I talk to my sister Tamiko about being biracial. She understands. Sometimes I get mad when people annoy me because I don't fit into a single category — Asian American or African American. I am both. I can tell her when I meet someone who is multiracial which makes me happy.

AKINA YOUNGE
WHITE PLAINS, NY
AGE 11

ANN UMEMOTO

I don't think there is anything wrong with being biracial. People say things about Blacks and Whites. I think they really don't know what color you are. Sometimes I feel hurt.

A couple summers ago, my Mom and I were shopping and this store had a sidewalk table set up with all kinds of beautiful wreaths. Mom asked me to go in and ask how much they were. My Mom was behind me. I got to the counter and asked. The man looked at me, then at my Mom and said they weren't for sale. We just looked at each other and walked away.

I was hurt, but I feel that man was ignorant. That was the last experience I had with something like that.

Colors do not matter to me. If someone made a racial comment to me it would go through one ear and out the other. There are people in my Mom's family that are racist. My sister and I used to talk about it and she and I think we don't see colors. I like all people. Just because you are a different color doesn't mean you are different. It's your character that matters.

All I have to say is if someone does make rude comments to you, don't! let it get to you. Just think about the good things about yourself. I am very proud of who I am because I have the best of both worlds.

MERCEDES DILLARD
COLUMBUS, OHIO
AGE 12

TANYA HUTCHINS

TANYA HUTCHINS

TANYA HUTCHINS

Mercedes Dillard & Chandel Charles
(Mercedes' Godmother is Chandel's
Grandmother)

I like the fact that I'm biracial. There are pros and cons... The pros are that you can have friends on both sides of your race you interact with. People make friends easy.

If you get down about your race, do what you feel is good and you like to do. I like to listen to my music when I get sad.

The cons are that people ask me "What color are you?" I say that "I'm mixed." They say, "I thought you were black because your Dad is black and your Mom is black." I say, "My Dad is not black, he's white." They say, "How is he white if he looks like it?" I say, "Because my grandmother and grandfather are white but he looks black because his great-grandfather is Indian." They say, "OK."

I've learned that your closest friends don't ask you what is your race, they just be your friend for who you are, not for your race.

ROGER KAZEE
COLUMBUS, OHIO
AGE 12

TANYA HUTCHINS

TANYA HUTCHINS

I am African-American, Hispanic, and Caucasian. I see myself mostly as African-American because that is what I look like.

Sometimes when my family has gone someplace where most people are of one race, people have looked at us funny (both of my parents are white because I am adopted). It used to bother me when people looked at me that way.

Kids at school would make fun of me. They would ask if "those people" were my parents even though they knew "those people" were. Eventually, I figured out that those people were ignorant of what family meant. Family is the people who take care of you and help you through troubled times. That relationship is forever. If bystanders can't figure that out, their opinion doesn't matter.

REBECCA BRESTEL
CINCINNATI, OHIO
AGE 12

TANYA HUTCHINS

When I was asked... to write something about being biracial, I couldn't think of anything at first. This is probably because I have great friends and people around me that accept me for who I am.

When I was younger, a boy came up to me and asked, "What are you?" I said that I was a girl with a great heart, and he said nothing and just turned away. So, the next time someone says something about your color, give them an answer like mine and see what they say and do.

In the past people have asked if I was adopted because I have a white mom and a black dad. I said, "No." They said that it couldn't be so. So I have told them that I wasn't black or white. One time when I said that to a boy he told me, "You're weird and stupid." I told him that I wasn't weird or stupid. I said that I was lucky and blessed to be the color that I am and to be both black and white, that the same God that made me made him.

After a while, I began to think of what I do that my parents have taught me to help me deal with people. I don't always listen to what people say, because every one is different in some way. If you are having trouble with certain people, then try to look at the friends you have and see if they are the ones saying things about you. If they are, then you may be hanging around with the wrong group of friends.

KELLEE MANUEL
URBANA, OHIO
AGE 12

42

   Try to find a different circle of friends that will accept you for who you are and support you. My parents told me that it's not what's on the outside that counts but what is on the inside. You can be beautiful on the outside but ugly and evil on the inside. In the same way a person can be not so pretty in their looks but have a beautiful heart.

   No one is perfect and every one of us is different.

KELLEE MANUEL
URBANA, OHIO
AGE 12

TANYA HUTCHINS

I haven't had really any experience of being known as a biracial girl. I have had one time my color actually mattered. My best friend has a grandpa who is prejudiced, and he doesn't like to see her hang out or be around blacks. So, one day my friend took me to his house without knowing he was this way. So, as I was in their house, I just smiled at him. But he gave me a very strange look with his face. I couldn't understand why he wasn't smiling back. When we left, my friend finally told me he was against blacks. I felt very bad. I don't know why I felt that way, but I hadn't done anything to him that was mean or disrespectful to make him dislike me. Later I found out that her grandpa yelled at her mother about me being in his house and that really hurt!

I just don't understand why people are this way! Everyone is supposed to be equal! God created all of us, not just some of us. So, I solved this by staying away from her grandpa's house because my friend and I can still have fun without going to his house. And I'm not going to let him get to me. So, what I learned from that situation is to stay away from people who are going to let my color get to them. It's not worth putting myself in a place that is going to cause me pain if I can avoid it.

ASHLEE MANUEL
URBANA, OHIO
AGE 13

44

Another thing, most of my friends are white, and their parents won't let them go out with or date biracial kids. That really makes me mad because it doesn't matter the person's outside color or looks! It's the inside that counts! So, when one of my friends likes a person of a different color, they have to break up with them or they get in trouble. I ask my friends why it matters and they told me that their parents told them it's because blacks and whites don't go together.

My advice to anyone in this situation is, think of all the famous, good, and smart people who are biracial and make a list of all the good things they have contributed to our world. Show them your list and tell your parents if it wasn't for these famous people's parents creating them, they wouldn't have been born to make the difference they did. Besides, I just give up or give in because someone doesn't like my skin color!

I am more than a color, I am smart, a good friend, a person who likes to help others, and beautiful (as I have been told so many times). I'm glad my parents created me. Maybe, I can make a difference in this world like other biracial people have.

ASHLEE MANUEL
URBANA, OHIO
AGE 13

I am biracial, my mother is white and my father is black. I'm glad I'm biracial. The way I see it is that I have the best of both worlds. I have never really had any major problems with being mixed. Kids have said stupid things to me, like calling me names, but it never really bothered me. I think kids just make issues of different races because they don't know anything about it. Some kids just have nothing else better to do with their time.

My advice to other biracial kids is to just ignore stupid comments that others have to say. If the issue still bothers you then maybe you should let your parents know so that they can contact that kid's parents. Then you can deal with the problem.

The last piece of advice I have is to be true to you. Don't let people put you down, they may just make you believe it. Be proud of who you are because everyone is special in their own way.

MARIE WHITE
RIVER ROUGE, MICHIGAN
AGE 13

DALE WHITE

Many people assume that when you're biracial   you have to choose. Well, we choose not to choose. As biracial people we get exposed to two worlds: we watch Grandma Edith make her delicious home- made apple sauce, and Grandma Terri make her sushi. Grandma Terri even converted her Japanese delicacy into a Japanese specialty, "Spam sushi."

For us there is no "other" half. Could you say your father is more important than your mother is? No. We don't say that one race is better than the other. We need both races to create our complete identity. There are hard parts too. Most people don't even think about where they fit in. But the question for us is, do we hang out with people of our father's race or people of our mother's race? Whenever we go on dates they will always be multiracial. We solved our dilemma by not worrying about what color skin other people have and what color skin we have. Our friends are people who would like us regardless of skin color. The most vital thing to remember is that for us it has never been and will never be fifty percent of one and fifty percent of the other. It's one hundred percent of both.

TAMIKO YOUNGE
WHITE PLAINS, NY
AGE 14

48

ABOUT THE AUTHOR

KIM JOHNSON

Tanya Hutchins is a freelance writer and reporter based in Washington, DC. She was a TV News Anchor/Reporter for 15 years in Columbus, OH. Tanya is a graduate of Ithaca College in Ithaca, New York, where her major was Television-Radio, with a concentration in Broadcast Journalism. Her minor was Anthropology. She is also an avid still photographer and some of her pictures are featured in this book.

While Tanya does not consider herself biracial, many of her ancestors were, so she embraces her multicultural heritage of African, European and Native American Indian ancestry.

Follow @TanyaHutchins on Twitter.

Made in the USA
San Bernardino, CA
08 November 2014